The Early Christian and Norse Settlements at BIRSAY

by C. A. RALEGH RADFORD

EDINBURGH
HER MAJESTY'S STATIONERY OFFICE

ISBN 0 11 491521 0

THE BROUGH OF BIRSAY

The Orkneyinga Saga—the Saga of the Men of Orkney—tells us that Earl Thorfinn the Mighty, who died about 1065, lived at Birsay and that the Bishop's seat was established there before its removal to Kirkwall in the middle of the twelfth century. Excavations have been carried out on the Brough of Birsay at various dates, starting in 1866; they are still in progress. The work has disclosed not only the remains of the Cathedral and residence of the eleventh and twelfth centuries, but of a whole sequence of earlier buildings. The structures already uncovered, in whole or in part, illustrate the varying fortunes of the early church in the Orkneys. The story starts with the coming of Christianity about A.D. 600 and ends soon after the middle of the twelfth century when the Cathedral was transferred to Kirkwall.

The remains on the Brough of Birsay fall into several phases. In the late sixth or early seventh century, when Christian missionaries first reached the islands, they formed part of the Pictish kingdom. The church then established followed the Celtic model, with an organization based on large monasteries; the earliest remains on the Brough belong to one of these monasteries. The Celtic church survived till the ninth century when the islands were settled by immigrants from West Norway. The newcomers were heathen and the ruined monastery at Birsay was replaced with a group of farmsteads, the earliest of which dates from the period of the Norse immigration. In time the Brough became one of the principal seats of the Earls of Orkney. A great dwelling house dating from the eleventh century is now being explored; it incorporates walls of another great building, going back to the tenth century. Earl Thorfinn was a Christian and about 1050, on his return from a pilgrimage to Rome, he built a 'splendid minster' at Birsay. Substantial remains of this church still stand to the west of the eleventh-century residence. In the early twelfth century Thorfinn's minster became the cathedral of Orkney. This transition is marked by certain alterations in the structure of the church and by the erection of an episcopal palace lying to the north. On the site of the residence, which had been burnt, arose a series of small dwellings, probably appropriated to the canons of the cathedral. Surrounding the church is an extensive graveyard in which two levels of burials can be distinguished, belonging respectively to the Pictish and the Norse periods.

HISTORY

THE BROUGH OF BIRSAY

The Celtic (or Pictish) Church

When St. Columba was at the court of Brude, the High King of the Picts, he asked this ruler to instruct the sub-king of the Orkneys to receive favourably St. Cormac and his companions, who had sailed north to seek a hermitage in the islands of the ocean. This intervention is said to have saved the missionaries from sudden death in the Orkneys. The episode, which is our earliest record of Christianity in the far north, must be dated to the last quarter of the sixth century when the great abbot and founder of Iona was carrying out his missionary activities among the northern Picts whose centre was then at Inverness.

St. Cormac and his companions were Irishmen from the Irish kingdom of Dalriada in Argyll. But there is no evidence of specifically Irish influences in the church which was then established in the Orkneys. The Celtic saints, whose names have survived in the northern islands, all come from the British or Pictish areas in Scotland, indicating the connections of the northern church in the days before the Norse settlement. They include St. Ninian [St. Ninian's Isle, Mainland of Shetland], the founder of the great British monastery at Whithorn in Galloway, and St. Triduana [St. Tredwell's Chapel on Papa Westray], a Pictish Abbess, also commemorated in Lothian. The existence of medieval chapels, named after these saints, shows that the missionaries, who established the church in the Orkneys, came from the Pictish kingdom and not from the region under the direct influence of Iona, the Irish kingdom of Dalriada in Argyll. The earliest memorials in the islands, the symbol stones, point to the same conclusion; they are typically Pictish. The great majority of monuments of this type are concentrated in the heartland of the old Pictish kingdom, the area east of the great mountains and lying between the Forth and the shores of the Moray Firth.

The organization of the Celtic church was based on a series of large monasteries, each providing for the religious needs of the surrounding district. The monks included priests responsible for the conversion of the inhabitants and the provision of religious services for the surrounding communities. Outside the monastery were sites set apart for religious purposes. These were originally enclosures marked

2

with a standing cross; later small chapels were built within the enclosures. In Orkney a number of the Norse chapels, the sites of which are recorded on many of the ouncelands, go back to the Pictish period.

A Celtic monastery consisted of an enclosure and a group of buildings within. The latter would include one or more small churches, buildings for common purposes, such as a school, a library and a scriptorium for the copying of manuscripts, or a guesthouse, and dwellings or cells for the monks, together with the barns and workshops needed by a community that was largely self-supporting. Such monasteries became centres of pilgrimage; they always included a cemetery, burial in which was a privilege much sought after.

The headland known as the Brough of Deerness on the east side of Mainland still retains the layout of an extensive Celtic monastery with a wall facing the landward edge of the cliff and forming the monastic enclosure. On the Brough of Birsay the ruins of a small church have been identified under the Norse Cathedral. It lay within a cemetery with its own enclosure wall. No other buildings of the monastery have yet come to light but there is an extensive burial ground which has yielded a broken symbol stone, an early cross and a fragmentary inscription in Ogam characters, showing that it was already established in the seventh or early eighth century.

Celtic Christianity laid particular stress on the value of the contemplative life for which the monks would retire, either temporarily or in old age, to a hermitage or retreat. These hermitages generally lay in remote places and its subsequent history suggests that there may have been one on the little island of Eynhallow [the holy island].

The Norse Immigration

Archaeology has revealed traces of the first Norse settlement in the Orkneys. The incomers were farmers from West Norway, probably seeking fresh lands to relieve the pressure of population at home. They were pagans and the grave goods which accompany their burials show that the immigration goes back to the first half of the ninth century.

On the Brough of Birsay this phase is reflected in the long houses which lie on the slope above the cathedral. Some of these are typical farms with the living quarters in the upper end and the byres for cattle in the lower part of the building. Two of them, now fully uncovered have the broad stone-faced walls of turf and the bowed outline with contracted ends that are found in farms belonging to the earliest period of Norse colonial expansion in the ninth century. The

3

type has recently been studied in detail in the settlement at Jarlshof in Shetland.

The Norse Earldom

The traditional account, recorded in the Orkneyinga Saga, connects the Norse settlement of Orkney with a grant of the islands to Earl Rognvald of Möre, in West Norway. The date indicated would be near the end of the ninth century. The grant is said to have been transferred to Earl Rognvald's brother, Sigurd, and there is no doubt that Earl Sigurd was ruling in Orkney about 900. He died during a campaign on the Scottish mainland and was buried near Dornoch.

The traditional account must be interpreted as referring to the establishment of the historical ruling house but there is no reason to accept the implication that this was associated with the beginnings of Norse colonisation, a conclusion that would be at variance with the archaeological evidence already mentioned. The Norse earls of Orkney were nominally subject to the kings of Norway but this suzerainty was not always effective.

The dynastic history of the Earls of Orkney is told with a wealth of vivid and poetic detail in the Orkneyinga Saga. It has often been retold and need not here be repeated in detail. Turf Einar, a base-born son of Earl Rognvald, dominates the story in the early tenth century. His great grandson, Earl Sigurd the Stout, was ruling in 995 when Olaf Tryggvason, King of Norway, came to the islands. One of the fiercest and most dreaded of the Viking rulers, he had recently been converted to Christianity. Inspired by missionary zeal he forced Earl Sigurd and his people to accept the new faith under a threat of death and devastation.

That Birsay was a seat of these Earls of Orkney is a reasonable conjecture. On the edge of the cliff, south of the later Earl's residence, are the remains of a great hall, not yet fully explored and in large part eroded by the sea. Since one end is incorporated in the eleventh century residence it must have been disused before 1050. It is a long house superficially resembling the farms already mentioned, but laid out on a larger scale and apparently without cattle stalls at the lower end. A similar building, partly explored on the island of Rousay, can reasonably be identified as the hall of the ancestors of Sigurd of Westness, a chieftain of the twelfth century. The longhouse at Birsay appears to be a hall even larger than that at Westness. This large size is probably to be explained by the need to accommodate the hird or bodyguard, which the Earls of Orkney probably retained on the model of their Norwegian suzerains.

Earl Sigurd the Stout died in 1014, in the great battle of Clontarf, outside Dublin. He was succeeded by his sons whose fratricidal strife occupies much of the history of the next thirty years. The youngest Thorfinn was at first excluded from the succession by reason of his youth. But he gradually gained the ascendancy and by the middle of the eleventh century he was the undisputed ruler of the Orkneys.

Thorfinn the Mighty was the most powerful of all the Earls of Orkney. Once firmly established he journeyed to Norway to visit his suzerain, King Harald Hadrada, and then went on to Denmark to the court of King Swegn. From Denmark he went to the Emperor Henry II; then south to Rome to visit the Pope from whom he obtained absolution for his sins. 'And this journey was most famous', comments the Saga writer. After his return to the north Earl Thorfinn, Lord of the Orkneys, of the Hebrides down to the Isle of Man, of nine earldoms in Scotland and of extensive lands in Ireland, gave up raiding and warfare and 'sat continually in Birsay', governing the islands. At Birsay he built Christchurch, 'a splendid minster'. The journey to Rome took place about 1050; Earl Thorfinn died some fifteen years later.

The plan and details of the church built on the Brough—more particularly the form of the quire, opening directly out of the nave, and the double splayed window in the north wall—are consistent with a date in the middle of the eleventh century. The church type closely corresponds with that of a number of Irish buildings of this age which are connected with monastic communities. An ecclesiastical community of the type concerned would then normally be known as a minster or monastery though later medieval custom would have referred to it as a house of secular canons.

Thorfinn's church stands within a rectangular wall enclosing the graveyard. On the slope below the graveyard, the remains of a great house have emerged from beneath the ruins of later buildings. Its well-built stone walls provide a striking contrast to turf walls of the farms and of the earlier hall. The great house is associated stratigraphically with the church and the objects recovered show that it dates from the eleventh century. Only a part of the building has yet been explored and much of it has been washed away by the encroachment of the sea, but the rooms already uncovered show that it was arranged on a centralised plan typical of the rather later great houses of the Norse world, such as the Bishop's Palace at Gardar in Greenland. That this building on the Brough of Birsay was the residence of Earl Thorfinn the Mighty would, in any circumstances, be a reasonable conclusion; its association with the contemporary church leaves no room for reasonable doubt.

St. Magnus and the Organisation of the Norse Church in Orkney

The years following Thorfinn's death saw a continuance of peaceful conditions in the Orkneys. His two sons, Earls Paul and Erlend, ruled the islands jointly and in amity. But the last years of the century brought rising dissensions among the next generation. At the same time King Magnus of Norway asserted his position in the islands and exiled the two earls. After the death of King Magnus the local dynasty was re-established in the person of Earl Hakon, son of Paul. But the claims of Magnus, the son of Earl Erlend, to a share in the inheritance led to a feud which culminated probably in 1117, in the brutal murder of Magnus on the island of Egilsay. His body was claimed by his mother, Thora, and buried in the minster on Birsay, the foundation of his grandfather, Earl Thorfinn.

Within a generation of his death and burial in the church at Birsay miracles were reported at the tomb of Earl Magnus. These reports were unwelcome to Earl Hakon and his supporters who did not fail to recognise the political implication of a resurgence of the defeated adherents of Earl Magnus. Bishop William, who now appears in the story for the first time, adopted a sceptical attitude which was doubtless imposed by the need to retain the favour of the reigning earl. But the stories multiplied and became more insistent and about 1135 the Bishop, yielding to the pressure of opinion, caused the body of Earl Magnus to be translated to a shrine and taken to Kirkwall. This recognition of the virtues of the murdered man provided the church in Orkney with a local saint whose memory is still preserved in the Cathedral at Kirkwall.

Bishop William died in 1168 and was reputed to have held the See of Orkney for 60 years. He is first mentioned as residing on the island of Egilsay, where St. Magnus had met his death. The roofless church of St. Magnus on that island is early Romanesque in character with a number of features modelled on Irish practice of the eleventh century. It was probably erected for the use of a small ecclesiastical community perhaps the household of the bishop; it is certainly older than 1135, when Bishop William is first mentioned, and may have been erected before 1117, the date of the martyrdom of St. Magnus. But there is no suggestion that this church ever served as the Cathedral of Orkney; that honour was reserved for the church on Birsay, erected by Earl Thorfinn.

The date of the establishment of this cathedral is not recorded. It may well have been when Bishop William came to the Orkneys; he is the first holder of the See known to have been resident in the islands. His arrival probably took place some years later than 1108, which is implied by his reputed 60-year tenure of the See. The choice of this church was a natural one. It was in Thorfinn's day the principal church in the islands and he probably designed it as the seat of a bishop whom he would have regarded much in the light of a chaplain attached to his court.

The change represented by the establishment of the bishopric at Birsay is clearly reflected in the buildings. The great residence of Earl Thorfinn—or at least the part so far explored, including the great hall—was burnt. Above the burnt ruins and in places incorporating its walls, is a series of small houses grouped together within an enclosure facing the church. The masonry is less pretentious and less finished than the older walls but the houses are well constructed dwellings and differ from the farmhouses in the absence of byres and workshops. They are the type of dwelling which one might expect to find occupied by the canons of the cathedral or other clergy attached to the bishop's household.

At the same time the church was modified. Two circular recesses, with altars served from small raised platforms, were inserted in the eastern angles of the nave. A second door was cut through the north wall of the nave, leading to an enclosed courtyard. The added altars imply an increase in the number of the ecclesiastical community serving the minster and their arrangement finds in nearest analogy in early Norse churches such as the Olafskyrrke at Trondheim and the rather later cathedral at Gardar in Greenland.

The buildings immediately north of the church are contemporary with these alterations. They are set over the north wall of the rectangular churchyard which is contemporary with the original minster and a paved path runs obliquely across the courtyard from the inserted north door of the cathedral to an entrance in the northwest angle. The buildings consist of three ranges, enclosing the courtyard, of which the fourth side is formed by the nave of the church. The main block on the north has a large eastern and a small western room. These are now separated by a passage but only the western wall of this passage is original. The arrangement suggests a hall with an ante-chamber at the west end. The earlier entrance, now blocked, was at the west end of the south wall, outside the western range. This was approached across the west side of the churchyard, which was kept free of graves, and the position of the main entrance to the churchyard was moved westward to provide more convenient access. The west range, entered from the antechamber, had one large room, probably the great chamber. The east range consisted of smaller rooms, probably storehouses. The whole complex is clearly a great dwelling house and the parallels suggest that it was the palace of the bishop, laid out in imitation of the more civilized episcopal palaces of the south. Its date must lie near the middle of the twelfth century.

Later History

In 1137 Earl Rognvald vowed the erection of a new and more magnificent cathedral in the settlement now known as Kirkwall. Work was quickly begun and the earliest parts of the new building— the western part of the existing quire and the transepts—are shown by their detail to belong to the middle of the twelfth century; it is probable that the new cathedral was sufficiently advanced to be used soon after 1150. When this happened Kirkwall replaced Birsay as the cathedral of the Diocese.

Birsay, none the less, remained an important church, serving one of the richest possessions of the medieval bishops. There is evidence of minor alterations to Earl Thorfinn's church during the thirteenth century and a number of later alterations can be traced in the bishop's palace. But the inconvenience of a residence on the small tidal islet must soon have made itself felt and a transfer to the mainland took place some time during the Middle Ages.

This transfer cannot be exactly dated. The present parish church of Birsay is a post-Reformation building but it incorporates a re-used window of the late thirteenth century. Built into the church and a neighbouring house are two pieces of a late medieval inscription which reads 'Mons Bellus'. The inscription is of a type that might well have been set over the door of a great house and Dr. Marwick has identified a letter of a sixteenth century Bishop of Orkney dated from Mons Bellus. It may be conlcuded that the later residence of the medieval bishops of Orkney lay on the mainland, on or near the site of the ruined sixteenth-century palace of Earl Robert Stewart.

The church on the Brough of Birsay doubtless remained in use down to the Reformation. It was frequented as a place of pilgrimage to an even later period. In 1627 the site was said to retain the 'foundation of ane kirk and kirkyard' which 'is thought by the elder to have belongit to the reid frieris'.

The site was first explored in 1866 by Sir Henry Dryden, who uncovered the walls of the church, and which became widely known from his work and from the account published by MacGibbon and Ross. The site of the church and the surrounding area were subsequently purchased by Mr. David Swan Wallace, and in 1936 were conveyed to the then Ministry of Works as an Ancient Monument. Extensive excavations were carried out by the Ministry before the War of 1939–45. These were necessarily suspended on the outbreak of war when the exposed and untreated remains of walling were temporarily covered to prevent deterioration. The excavations were restarted in 1956 and are now proceeding together with the consolidation of the buildings.

The Identification of the Church on the Brough of Birsay

The Orkneyinga Saga calls the church erected by Earl Thorfinn at Birsay Christchurch. Post-Reformation tradition names the ruined building on the Brough after St. Peter or, less authoritatively, St. Columba or St. Colme. It has therefore been argued that there were two separate churches and that the site on the islet could not have been the minster of Thorfinn. The question has further been complicated by the reference in 1627 attributing the ruins to the Red Friars.

The second point can be summarily dismissed. The Red Friars, or, to give them their proper designation, the Order of the Trinitarians for the Redemption of Slaves, were founded by Pope Innocent III [1198–1216] and did not reach Scotland till the middle of the thirteenth century. Except for minor alterations all the work on the Brough was completed before 1200. The plan of the Bishop's Palace has no more than a superficial resemblance to that of a monastic house. Moreover the only secure reference to property at Birsay owned by this Order concerns land on the mainland, not the islet.

The argument based on the name of the church, though apparently more cogent, rests on a misconception. In the early period, before the twelfth century, Christian churches were dedicated to Christ and named after a saint the founder or often the principal saint, of whom a relic was enshrined in the building. Thorfinn's 'most famous' journey to Rome was the prelude to his building the minster at Birsay. At Rome he 'saw the Pope and there he took absolution from him for all his misdeeds'. The foundation of the minster was certainly agreed upon while the Earl was in Rome and it is inconceivable that he did not bring back with him a relic of the Prince of the Apostles whose tomb he would visit as a part of the normal routine of a pilgrimage to Rome. This relic may not have been corporeal; the older Roman practice was to take pieces of silk, hallow them by contact with the tomb of St. Peter, then place the silk in a small casket, or pyx, for enshrinement in the church, normally in a cavity within the main altar. The church would then, to paraphrase the Saxon documents, be 'dedicated to Christ with the name of St. Peter'. In later centuries the looser phrase dedicated to St. Peter would become normal.

DESCRIPTION

The Brough of Birsay is a tidal islet barely 804 metres across, lying off the northwest point of the Mainland of Orkney. It is reached by a rough track leading from the village along the shore of the bay to a point from which a modern causeway crosses the gap of 109 metres separating the islet from the mainland; the passage on foot can only be made at low tide. In the early Christian period the crossing was certainly narrower but there can be no suggestion that the passage over the jagged rocks would have been any easier than it was before the construction of the causeway.

Leaving the causeway the visitor climbs up a steep path which rises in a slight cleft in the low cliff forming the landward side of the islet. Immediately in front is the modern stone-built Museum and office. To the right, in front of the Museum, is the Churchyard with the walls of the Cathedral and the Bishop's Palace beyond. Below these, between the Churchyard and the edge of the cliff, are the later Norse dwellings, built into the ruins of the dwelling, which is not yet fully explored. Higher up the slope, above and beyond the Churchyard is a series of separate farms extending up to, and in one place beyond, the boundary fence.

The Cathedral

The Cathedral consists of a small rectangular nave and a narrower, almost square, quire with an apse on the east side. The original walling is formed of roughly split rubble. The jambs of the doors, the quoins and other details are formed of rather larger stones. On either side of the west door two series of projecting stones or tuskers mark the spring of the side walls of a porch. The heavy foundations, still visible in the ground, suggest that this was designed as the base of a western tower. No trace of such a building remains and the position of the later entrance to the Bishop's Palace, set in the southwest corner of the courtyard, suggests that it was never built. The only other original details in the cathedral are the window in the north wall of the quire, where the masonry still stands to a height of about 2·3 metres and traces of another window on the north side of the apse.

2 The Cathedral: in the distance, the mainland of Orkney

3 South side of the Cathedral, Norse cemetery wall in foreground

The Norse Cathedral
and Bishop's Palace

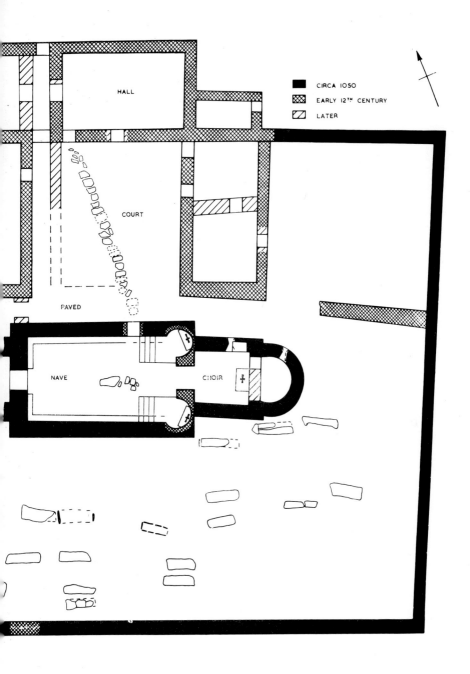

HALL

CIRCA 1050

EARLY 12ᵀᴴ CENTURY

LATER

COURT

PAVED

NAVE

CHOIR

5   10   15 metres

5 The antechamber and hall (left) of the Bishop's Palace. The courtyard, and
   church beyond, are to the top right of the picture

6   Norse houses: in the distance is Marwick Head

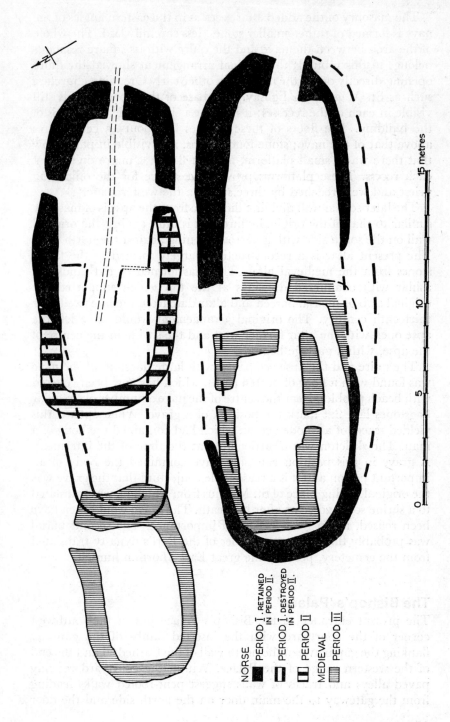

NORSE

■ PERIOD I. RETAINED IN PERIOD II.

▨ PERIOD I. DESTROYED IN PERIOD II.

▤ PERIOD II.

MEDIEVAL

▨ PERIOD III

15 metres

10

5

0

The masonry of the added altar recesses in the eastern angles of the nave is formed of rather smaller stones, less carefully laid. The whole of the arch between the nave and the quire with its square responds belongs to this rebuild; the original arrangement showed the quire opening directly out of the nave, as in other early Orcadian churches, such as St. Magnus on Egilsay. The base of the stone altar is still visible in each of the recesses; it is set at a slight angle to the axis of the building. The floors of these recesses lie about 45 centimetres above that of the nave; stone foundations, still visible in part, show that there was a small platform, about 1·8 by 1·2 metres in front of each recess. These platforms provided a stance for the officiating priest and were reached by three steps on the western side.

The later screen wall dividing the quire from the apse is of masonry similar to that of the original church. It is built against the original wall on the south side with a narrow opening against the north wall. The present altar is a reconstruction, largely formed of the fallen stones from the medieval altar. This was formed of red sandstone ashlar with chamfered dressings at the top which supported the original slab or mensa. Screen and altar date from the late twelfth or thirteenth century. The original arrangement would have left the apse open with the altar further west and the shrine in the centre of the apse, with a passage behind.

The quire and the apse are paved with large flagstones. The nave was found with a floor of beaten earth, which has now been covered with beach pebbles. Near the centre of the nave a number of irregular flagstones laid flat mark the position of a grave. When opened this yielded traces of a wooden coffin which had contained the body of a man. The skeleton was disarticulated at the time of the interment. A grave in this position can only have contained the body of an important person and it is a reasonable conjecture that the grave was the original resting place of St. Magnus from which he was translated to a shrine some 20 years after his death. The grave would then have been reused, again for a person of importance. The second burial was probably that of some member of the Earl's dynasty translated from the cemetery, possibly the great Earl Thorfinn himself.

The Bishop's 'Palace'

The present entrance to the Bishop's Palace lies in the southwest corner of the courtyard with the inserted jambs of the gateway flanking the gap between the north wall of the Cathedral and the end of the western range of the Palace. Within the courtyard roughly paved alleys and traces of walls suggest pent-roofed walks leading from the gateway to the main door on the north side and the door into the church. These are later arrangements. Originally there was only a path formed of a line of irregular slabs running obliquely across from the main door to the church.

The Bishop's Palace consists of three ranges of buildings almost enclosing the central courtyard of which the north wall of the cathedral forms the fourth side. The principal range is that on the north with its main entrance in the northwest corner of the courtyard. The door leads into a narrow passage which extends across the building to a back door, beyond which lay the kitchen and other domestic offices, which are only explored in part. The wall on the right of the passage is original with a central doorway leading into the main room. This was the Bishop's Hall, the passage corresponding to the screens of the normal medieval house. The wall on the left of the passage is an insertion, possibly replacing an earlier partition of timber. It has a smaller central doorway, the opening in the original wall on the opposite side of the passage being later narrowed to correspond. To the west of the passage is another large room. In a normal medieval house this would form the service rooms, the buttery and pantry. In the later period this space, subdivided by wooden partitions, may have been used for this purpose. The original arrangement was different. Two large blocked doors can be traced in the south wall; one led to the west range, the other to the open enclosure beyond that range. The latter was certainly the original entrance, before the gateway was inserted in the space between the cathedral and the palace. The former leading into the west range, the Bishop's private apartments, suggests that the western room was intended as an antechamber, the place, where persons seeking audience with the Bishop or attending his court could wait till they were received. This is borne out by the fact that the clay subsoil in the centre of this room was burnt to a dark red by a long series of fires; this does not suggest a kitchen but rather the fire which would be kept burning in the antechamber. In the southeast corner of this room was a block of tumbled rubble, now removed, suggesting the base of a staircase to an upper floor of the west range.

The west range consists of a single large apartment with a separate entrance from the courtyard; it probably formed the Camera or Private Chamber of the Bishop. This apartment may have lain on the first floor, in which case the lower stage may have served as the Bishop's Court, but the exact functions must remain uncertain. The small rooms in the east range, which have few details surviving were probably service or store rooms.

The Cemetery

A rectangular wall encloses the Norse Cemetery. The present entrance, near the west end of the south side, lies opposite the older, blocked door into the main range of the Palace. It was formed when the Palace was first built, replacing an older blocked entrance further east in the same wall.

The graves in the cemetery are at two levels. The upper series are marked by heavy cover stones, often thick weathered rectangular blocks of a hard grey slate. These stand well above the present surface and correspond to a ground level some 30 to 45 centimetres higher, when they would have projected only a few centimetres. These graves are Norse and belong to the period after the building of Earl Thorfinn's Cathedral. Graves of this series are found only to the south and east of the Cathedral showing that the west side of the cemetery was reserved as a passage leading to the Palace, which covers the whole north side of the enclosure, forming the original cemetery. It was probably to compensate for the space lost when the Palace was built that a new cemetery was added on the east side. This can still be traced with a few graves marked with flat cover slabs. The small number of graves in this added enclosure probably indicates that the new church on the mainland, represented by the modern parish church, was founded and brought into use for normal burials at an early date.

The lower and older series of graves is Pictish. The surface of the cemetery has been cleared down to this earlier level, exposing the tops of the slabs set on edge to form these graves. Many of these graves had small head or foot stones, the broken stumps of which sometimes remain. These earlier graves extend over the whole area outside the Palace, including the western strip, left free by the Norse; in this area the stumps of the headstones are all broken at a low level so that they would not have projected above the surface of the Norse period.

Two monuments in the earlier level of the cemetery call for special notice. On the south side, near the older blocked entrance into the Norse Cemetery, is a triple grave; the enclosing slabs are clearly visible. At the west end of this monument were found the broken fragments of a Pictish symbol stone, engraved with a naturalistic eagle, three conventional symbols and three human figures. There can be no doubt that this stone originally stood erect at the head of the triple grave and that it commemorated the three men buried there. They were probably high officers of the Pictish sub-king of the Orkneys. The second monument has been badly disturbed by later burials. It lies near the triple grave already described but rather nearer the Norse Cathedral. A row of stones about 2·4 metres long and running east and west, with a curved angle and a slight return at the west end, is all that can now be seen. These stones formed the kerb of a mound, probably some 2·4 metres square. The grave near the centre belongs to the later series and will have destroyed whatever lay at the centre of the older monument. Raised graves of this kind are known from other Celtic Christian cemeteries. They consist of a stone revetted mound up to 2·4 metres square and some 0·6 metres high, surmounted by a pillar stone carved with a cross. They were used to mark the burials of important ecclesiastics, such as the founder of a Celtic monastery.

The extent of the Pictish cemetery is not yet defined, except on the east side. The line of a roughly circular wall can be seen passing under the southeast corner of the Norse cemetery and running along the nearer side of the eastern Norse extension. This is a part of the enclosure wall of the Pictish cemetery. To the same period must be ascribed the remains of earlier walling underlying the south side of the nave of the Norse Cathedral. This masonry stands to a height of two or three courses and was already ruined in the eleventh century. It belongs to the older Pictish church.

To the east of the Norse cemetery lies a rectangular extension with a few graves, marked with flat slabs, on the south side. Other irregular enclosures of uncertain purpose may be seen outside the southeast corner of the cemetery.

In the course of clearing the cemetery area stones bearing fragments of Runic inscriptions were found. Two of these had been split longitudinally and reused as building material in the earliest part of the Cathedral.

The Norse Dwellings east of the Cathedral

Between the east side of the cemetery and the edge of the cliff lies a large complex of buildings, which was partly uncovered before the war and is still in process of exploration. It is not yet possible to give a full account of this part of the site and this part of the present guide is confined to a summary of the results obtained up to the end of the season of 1957.

The earliest feature yet identified in this area is an extensive kitchen midden with many crushed fragments of sea shells. The few objects found in this midden come from the upper layers. It is possible that it accumulated during the occupation of the Pictish monastery, the site of which has not yet been located, but it may be of much earlier date. The midden has been tested in trial pits and is nowhere visible.

Set into the surface of the midden is one Norse house [and possibly others] of the same type as those found on the slopes above the cemetery. The building has stone-faced walls of turf and its construction and stratigraphical position suggest an early date, probably in the ninth century. This house is only uncovered in part and its full plan is not yet established. It is possible that other structures will be found at this level as the lower strata are explored.

To the next stage belongs a large building with stone-faced walls of turf, running north and south on the southeast corner of the site. It is not yet fully explored and not marked on the plan. Only the north end remains, the rest of the building having been eroded by the sea. This end has a central doorway, flanked by swollen terminals which have been incorporated into the later Bath House [p. 16]. A considerable stretch of the long western wall is visible either exposed or as a turf covered mound. The outer, eastern, wall has almost entirely disappeared. The building is a large and substantial example of the typical Norse dwelling. Given the later history of the site it is possible that it represents the hall of the earlier Norse Earls who were ruling the islands at the end of the ninth and during the tenth centuries.

The third stage comprises a very extensive building, still in process of exploration. It appears to consist of a number of long rooms running east and west. The walls are of large stones set in clay and the floors are paved. Near the centre of the complex a part of one of these rooms has been exposed within one of the later rooms of the last stage. At the upper or west end the wall can be seen, lying partly under the later masonry and with the jamb of a door at the south end. On the north side of the room is a raised bench of earth with a kerb of stones set on edge. The older wall can be seen again on the south side. On the east side is a covered water channel with a small open basin. The water channel in its original form antedates the room; it was then open and the covering slabs mark its incorporation into the building. Two of these slabs can be seen forming the base of the bench.

The east wall of the late room, in which these remains have been exposed, lies on the older east wall of the lower room. Beyond this was another paved room. In this area the lower pavement represents the early floor. In the southeast corner is a contemporary firepit. Further to the east is a third room, part of which has been eroded by the sea [marked EARLY FLOOR on plan]. This room has a central firepit, the stones of which have been reddened by burning. The centre of the room is paved with large slabs. Along the three remaining sides run raised dais, paved with slabs, originally set about 45 centimetres above the central area. Beneath each dais is a heating channel, those on the south and west leading back to the firepit in the corner of the room to the west. The principal entrance to this heated room is in the northwest corner, leading down from another paved room with a central firepit. There was a further door on the south side, which led out to a paved courtyard crossed by a covered water channel. Only the west jamb of this doorway survives; it now lies about 30 centimetres from the edge of the cliff. Beyond this courtyard lies the bath house. The north side incorporating the end of the earlier hall has an externally curved wall. The other sides have thin walls of masonry against which banks of turf were piled to conserve the heat. The interior is divided by stone slabs set on edge. These bath houses were heated and water dashed on the hot stones to provide a vapour bath.

The objects associated with this large building date it to the eleventh century. The masonry of the rooms on the cliff edge, where it is best preserved, resembles that used in the Cathedral. This resemblance and the elaboration of the plan and detail, particularly the heating system, show that the erection must be attributed to Earl Thorfinn the Mighty and that it was his residence. The room with the raised dais is the festival hall or banqueting hall.

The fourth and final stage on the site is that shown on the plan. The complex consists of many small rooms with stone and turf walls and roughly paved floors. The plan suggests that we have to do with a number of small separate houses set within an enclosure facing the Cathedral. The technical achievement is far below that of Thorfinn's residence; many of the stones are rounded boulders from the beach used in place of the quarried and roughly split blocks of the preceding period. A characteristic feature of several of these rooms is the central fireplace formed of stone slabs set on edge. A good example is visible on the north side where the floor has been restored.

These houses were built over the ruins of Thorfinn's residence. The great hall of the earlier building was covered by a deep layer of peat ash into which the walls of a typical small house were set. [This is marked on the plan, but has now been removed, the fireplace being reset alongside the Museum]. Stratigraphically these houses belong to the twelfth century and are contemporary with the extension of the cemetery. It is reasonable to connect them with the episcopal household and regard them as the dwellings of the Bishop's priests or officials.

South of this site, on the cliff edge, can be seen the wide paved ramp and the roughly walled sides of a slipway for drawing up ships; the outer part has been cut away by the sea.

The Norse Houses

On the slope above the Cathedral are a number of separate buildings of various types. The greater number have stone-faced walls of turf and the plans resemble those normal in Norse lands between the ninth and thirteenth centuries. There are also a few small buildings, apparently of mortared masonry; some of these lie over ruined structures of the more normal type. Not all of these buildings have been fully explored. A detailed account of the two largest buildings follows; they lie on the south side of the enclosure and one of them passes under the modern boundary fence. These two buildings appear to be among the earliest of the whole group. They were uncovered before the war and sections dug across them in 1956 and 1957 in order to elucidate details of the plan and sequence.

The northern and nearer of the two buildings is the better preserved. It was originally a long house with thick walls of turf, faced on the inner side with a revetment of drystone masonry; the outer face of alternate courses of flat stones and turves has largely collapsed. The lower part of the house, below the doors in the long side walls, retains the original structure. Above these doors the walls have been rebuilt. The house originally extended further up the slope and the original end can be traced by the few stones which remain projecting above the present ground level. On the south side of the house the base of the original wall can be seen within the later wall, serving as a low bench.

The house originally measured 17·1 metres long with a maximum internal width of 4·6 metres, the long side walls being bowed outwards. There were doors opposite each other rather below the centres of the long sides and a third axially placed in the lower end.

The upper part of the house formed the living quarters. These are marked off by two rectangular spaces, delimited by stone slabs set on edge, and separated by a narrow paved passage; this passage continues down the long axis to pass through the doorway at the lower end. The rectangular spaces with their delimiting slabs formed the bases of enclosed wooden beds. In the centre of the living quarters the natural clay floor was burnt red by a long succession of fires, but there was no built hearth. The lower part of the building was a byre in which the cattle were tethered against the side walls; there is a covered drain beneath the central paved passage. The lower corner on the north side was paved and had an anvil of stone set in the floor.

The upper end and the south wall of this house collapsed outwards owing to the decay of the courses of turf on the outer face of the wall. They were then rebuilt with the outer sides entirely stone faced; these bases remain today. In the process the house was shortened by 4·9 metres.

The southern house was originally of the same type as the earlier building already described. The structure had been badly denuded and damaged by later ploughing but the essential features of the plan can be recovered. This house was also rebuilt but the visible remains belong almost entirely to the older structure. The space between the two houses, which are parallel and separated by only a metre or so, and an area below the lower ends were paved with large stone slabs in order to prevent rainwash and the consequent undercutting of the walls.

These two houses are typical examples of Norse farmhouses. They closely resemble those fully explored by the Department at Jarlshof on the Mainland of Shetland, where a full report has been published. The bowed shape of the side walls and the turf construction are features that occur as early as the ninth century both on that site and in Iceland. At Birsay the early date is borne out by the absence of pottery, which first became usual in the far north in the twelfth century and by the few artifacts recovered from these houses. In addition there is the historical argument that these large farms are likely to antedate the period when the Norse Earls chose Birsay as the site of their residence.

Over the upper ends of these houses are two small rectangular buildings of stone, probably set in clay. The more southerly is placed within the southern Norse farm while the other incorporates the destroyed upper end of the original northern house. These two buildings were erected at a time when the Norse farmhouses were ruinous and apparently forgotten. There is no dating evidence but the simple plan suggests cottages or sheds belonging to an agricultural establishment attached to the Bishop's Palace of the twelfth or thirteenth century.

On historical grounds it is likely that the other larger Norse buildings on the slope above the Cathedral also belong to the early period before the establishment of the Earls' seat at Birsay. The large halls with outshots, which can be distinguished on the ground, belong to a type which is found in the early Norse colonial period in Iceland and Greenland and should be dated as early as the tenth or eleventh century.

BIBLIOGRAPHY

A. W. BROGGER. *Ancient Emigrants*. Oxford, 1929.

STEWART CRUDEN. *The Early Christian and Pictish Monuments of Scotland*. HMSO, 1957.

J. R. C. HAMILTON, *Excavations of Jarlshof, Shetland*. HMSO, 1956.

H. MARWICK. *Orkney* [County Books], London: Robert Hale, 1951.

ROYAL COMMISSION ON HISTORICAL MONUMENTS, SCOTLAND. *Orkney and Shetland*. HMSO, 1946.

F. T. WAINWRIGHT [ed.]. *The Northern Islands*, 1962.

Printed in Scotland by Her Majesty's Stationery Office at HMSO Press, Edinburgh
Dd 403082 HF3161 K80 3/78 (14868)

Ancient Monuments and Historic Buildings

Many ancient sites and buildings are maintained as national monuments by the Department of the Environment.

Guide-books or pamphlets are on sale at many monuments and are also obtainable from the bookshops of Her Majesty's Stationery Office.

Postcards can be purchased at many monuments, or from the Clerk of Stationery, Department of the Environment, Argyle House, Lady Lawson Street, Edinburgh EH3 9SD, (Chief Information Officer, Department of the Environment, 2 Marsham Street, London SW1, for English and Welsh monuments).

Photographs of most monuments may be obtained in large prints at commercial rates, plus postage, from the Photographic Librarian, Department of the Environment, Argyle House, Lady Lawson Street, Edinburgh EH3 9SD, (Photographic Librarian, Department of the Environment, Hannibal House, London SE1, for English and Welsh monuments).

Season tickets, valid for 12 months from date of issue, admitting their holders free of charge to all ancient monuments and historic buildings in the care of the Department of the Environment in Scotland, England and Wales, may be obtained from the Department or at many monuments.

Her Majesty's Stationery Office

Government Bookshops

13a Castle Street, Edinburgh EH2 3AR
49 High Holborn, London WC1V 6HB
41 The Hayes, Cardiff CF1 1JW
Brazennose Street, Manchester M60 8AS
Southey House, Wine Street, Bristol BS1 2BQ
258 Broad Street, Birmingham B1 2HE
80 Chichester Street, Belfast BT1 4JY

*Government publications are also available
through booksellers*

ISBN 0 11 491521 0

Water Voles

by

Ruth Street

Published by Street Country 2011
www.street-country.com
ruth@street-country.com

Text by Ruth Street

Photos:
Inside back cover by Greg Webb
Page 9 water vole baby by Ralph Sambrook
Page 11 water vole and page 12 fox by Sarah Street
All other photos and illustrations by Ruth Street

Map on page 21 based on information from:
Water Vole Conservation Handbook Second Edition by Rob
Strachan and Tom Moorhouse published by
The Wildlife Conservation Research Unit 2006.
Manhood Wildlife and Heritage Group water vole survey
map 2010 *funded by* the Environment Agency.

Design by Ruth Street and Kevin Misselbrook
Artwork produced by Border Digital Ltd

Published by Street Country 2011
www.street-country.com

Acknowledgements
With thanks to my husband John, Claire Watkins, Fran Southgate
and all my other family, friends and colleagues who have
given their support and encouragement.

With special thanks to Dr. Jill Sutcliffe and Helen Lambert for editing the text.
Jill chairs the Manhood Wildlife and Heritage Group
and Helen is a retired teacher.

Contents

What are water voles?

Water voles are small mammals that live in and around water.

They are around 30 cm long including their tail and weigh up to 320 grams.

Their bodies are well adapted for life in and out of the water.

They have reddish brown fur with a dense coat of soft underfur to keep them warm. The outer coat has coarser, thicker hairs which shed water more easily and keeps them waterproof. The two layers together also trap air which helps to keep them warm and dry.

When they dive and swim they use their feet as paddles. A flap of skin inside their ears keeps water out.

They look similar to a rat but have rounder faces, with furry ears and tail.

An adult water vole is about the size of a small guinea pig and could fit in your hand.

Habitat - where water voles live

Water voles live in wetland habitats where there are clean, slow-flowing streams, ditches, rivers or ponds. It is important that there is water in them all year round, as they never go far from water.

They dig their burrows in the sides of waterways with steep muddy banks. They use their feet and teeth to make entrances to their burrows above and below the water and also in the top of the bank near the water's edge.

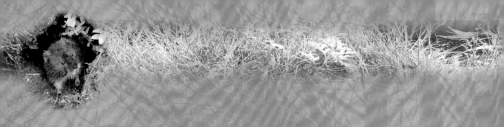

They need plenty of plants growing on the banks for food to eat and they use them as cover to hide from predators. As they run backwards and forwards between their holes, they make tunnels through the vegetation on the edge of the bank.

Water vole holes

Water vole tunnel

Collecting food

Water voles are mainly herbivores and use their sharp, orange teeth to feed on many different kinds of waterside plants. These include reeds, sedges, willow and grass. These grow best where there are gently sloping banks.

Their sharp teeth can cut pieces of plants at an angle which makes the stems pointed at one edge. They chop the stems into short lengths and store the pieces in a pile called a feeding station. Their front teeth grow all the time but all the chopping and cutting of plants wears them down and keeps them the same length.

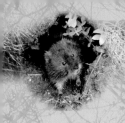

Cut stems

Feeding station

Sedge

Sometimes they eat all the plants in the area around their burrow so that it looks as if it has been cut by a lawn mower.

Reeds

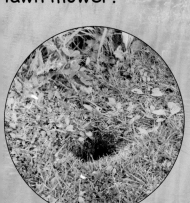
Water vole lawn

In winter, when there are less plants to eat, they feed mainly on the bark of trees and roots.

Droppings - keeping clean

Water voles keep their burrows clean by removing their droppings. They leave them in a pile in the same place every day called a latrine. The droppings are small, long and rounded at the ends. They are greenish brown as they are full of small pieces of plants and do not smell unpleasant.

Remember. do not touch animal droppings and always wash your hands after exploring animal habitats.

Reproduction - water vole families

Water voles breed from spring to autumn and usually have from 2-5 babies and up to 5-8 litters a year. The young are born underground in a nest lined with grass and rushes. They are blind and hairless when they are first born and only weigh 5 grams. When they are first born they feed on their mother's milk. They grow quickly and are covered in fur by the time they are 5 days old. They open their eyes when they are 7 days old and are ready to leave their mother after 3 weeks.

Water vole burrow

Water vole carrying baby in its mouth

One family will usually occupy about 70 metres

along the edge of a stream. The males often inhabit a stretch of bank 130 metres long as they often mate with more than one female.

Each family has 3 chambers in their burrow. One of these is the nest where the babies are born. The second chamber is where they live and the third is where they store food.

Males have scent glands on the side of their bodies. They rub their feet over them so they can mark their territory. The smell tells other

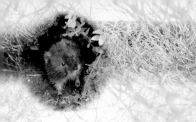

water voles that the stretch of bank and stream belongs to them. If they meet another male, they often fight to protect their territory.

Most water voles live for less than a year but sometimes they can live for 2-3 years.

They do not hibernate in winter but they spend more time in their burrows. Many of them die in the cold weather but enough usually survive to start breeding again in the spring.

It is important that they reproduce successfully each year, as they do not live very long. Otherwise, eventually they would die out.

Predators - water voles in danger

Water voles need to find plenty of plants to feed on each day to stay fit and healthy. But they also have to watch out for predators that would like to catch and eat them!

Fox

Animals such as foxes will catch water voles on land. Herons are birds that wade in the water watching for prey which they can stab with their long beaks. Pike are fish that find water voles make a tasty meal!

When water voles are being chased, they sometimes kick up mud from the bottom of the stream to confuse their predator. This makes the water cloudy so that they can't be seen and gives them time to escape.

Heron

Most predators are only able to catch water voles when they are outside their burrows.

But the worst predators are mink. These animals were brought from America and bred for their fur on farms. Mink are small, have very sharp teeth and are very fierce creatures. When the farms were closed down, many mink were released into the wild where many of them now live successfully. Mink are able to swim and are slim enough to be able to get into a water vole's burrow and then to kill the whole family. They can wipe out the whole population in an area.

Mink

Habitat loss - water voles in danger

Many places that were once good habitats for water voles have been destroyed.

Some streams, ditches and ponds have been filled in, dried out or become polluted.

In some places large machines have been used to clear out streams or ditches to improve the flow of water. But this has destroyed the plants on the banks so there is no food or shelter.

The banks of some streams, ditches and rivers have been reinforced with concrete to stop them washing away. But this means water voles cannot dig tunnels in the banks to make their burrows.

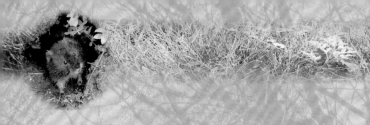

Sometimes farm animals eat the plants and trample the banks, which may destroy their burrows.

As water voles always live near water, flooding in winter or drought in summer can sometimes make it hard for them to survive.

The destruction of water vole habitat has meant that there are no longer many suitable places left where water voles can live.

Conservation – helping water voles

For an animal to survive it must have food, water, shelter, safety and somewhere to raise a family successfully. To prevent an endangered animal becoming extinct, it needs to be protected and the habitat where it lives must be looked after.

Water voles are endangered. Many have died out in the last 30 years because either they have been killed by mink or their habitat has become polluted or been destroyed.

90% of the water vole population has been destroyed in the last 30 years. This means that in an area where there used to be 100 water voles, 90 of them have died and there are now only 10 left.

If there are only a few water voles left in an area, a water vole may not be able to find a mate and breed successfully. Also predators or changes such as drought or flooding may wipe out the whole population. If there are more of them in an area, some of the water voles would be more likely to survive.

However people are trying to help water voles. In some places they are looking after their habitats and they also try to ensure there are no mink around which could kill them. People who own land such as farmers can help water voles too. They have to clear plants from their ditches so that rain water can drain away and the land does not flood. But if they leave some of the plants then water voles have

food and shelter and can live there too. Some conservation groups help by counting the water vole population. They go out and look for signs of water voles, especially water vole droppings and cut stems that they have chewed!

In some places where conditions are good and there are signs of water voles, the habitat is being looked after, to make sure it is not destroyed and that water voles can breed successfully.

There are now laws to fully protect water voles and their habitats.

Water mint

Enjoying wetlands

Wetland habitats are important for a wide range of plants and animals. They are also important for people! Where there is a healthy community of water voles, it shows that it is a healthy wetland where many other plants and animals can survive. We need to do what we can to help look after and protect these wonderful places!

Damselfly nymph

Dragonfly

Stickleback

Sussex case study

Water Voles in West Sussex – case study by Manhood Wildlife and Heritage Group

In 2000 a study was carried out in the Chichester area. The only surviving population of water voles in West Sussex was found on the Manhood Peninsula, which is the area around Pagham and Chichester Harbours and the farmland in between. But even this population was small and isolated and therefore under threat.

Why is the Manhood Peninsula so special?

This area of West Sussex is a flat coastal plain where the soil is very fertile. The climate is good for growing vegetables, salad and arable crops as there are long hours of sunshine. Many wildlife habitats are mixed in with the farming. The coastal grazing and tidal areas of the Harbours provide nesting and feeding sites for a large range of ducks, geese and wading birds and are also very important areas for plants and other wildlife. The farmland is crisscrossed by a network of waterways, including the Chichester Canal, streams and smaller ditches. These provide important habitat for water voles.

How do we know where they are?

Over the last 15 years regular surveys have taken place to look for the signs of water voles along the waterways. This has involved safely climbing into the waterways looking for burrows, latrines and feeding stations. On Chichester canal volunteers have used kayaks to look at the banks and under the vegetation. This information has been collected and studied to see where water voles are

living and to get an idea of the size of the population and which areas they like best.

What can we do to help the water vole?

The American mink is a non native species, which has been eradicated on the Manhood Peninsula by monitoring and trapping. The water vole has found the ditches, streams and waterways that cross farmland to be their best place to live. It was also discovered that water voles live in brackish pools (a mixture of salt and fresh water). Some of the farmers and landowners have put in place simple measures such as digging new ponds and protecting banks from cattle so their land is a good place for water voles to live. By 2003 the population of water voles on

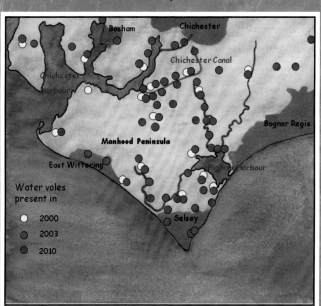

the Manhood Peninsula had tripled and by 2010 they had spread out to colonise more waterways in the area.

The future

Careful management of the waterways of the Manhood Peninsula and continuing control of mink should mean that the water vole population can have permanent homes here and may then disperse further afield. By making sure there is always habitat suited to water voles it will help other animals and plants and we may even get new species move into the area, such as the otter.

The aims of the Manhood Wildlife and Heritage Group are to: research, conserve and enhance the landscape, biodiversity and heritage of the Manhood Peninsula (the 11 Parishes which lie to the south of Chichester) through community involvement. It is a not-for-profit volunteer organisation.

The group began in 1997 by mapping the semi natural vegetation of the Parish of Selsey and became MWHG in 2004. In 2010, the group was awarded the Queen's Award for Voluntary Service, an equivalent to an MBE for groups. Part of its work includes working to safeguard the native population of water voles on the peninsula, the only such population in West Sussex.

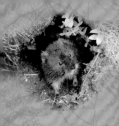

Water voles are one of Britain's fastest declining native mammals. The population has declined by 90% in the last 30 years.

The most famous water vole was 'Ratty' in the book 'Wind in the Willows' by Kenneth Grahame. Although he was called Ratty he was a water vole.

Water voles eat over 200 different types of plants. Their favourites include reeds, rushes and sedges in summer and willow and hawthorn bark in winter.

They have to eat the equivalent of 80% of their body weight a day, which is 60 – 360 grams of food, depending on their size.

They can climb trees and have been seen 2.5 metres above the ground.

Water voles can be confused with the brown rat. The water vole's tail is about half of its

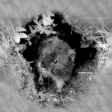

Water vole facts

body length and hairy and it also has a round face and furry ears. A rat is slightly larger, has a pointed nose and a tail that is much longer and looks naked or scaly.

If you listen quietly and watch carefully where water voles live, you may be able to see one. Sometimes you hear a 'plop' as they dive into the water, or a rustle like a packet of crisps as they move through the vegetation beside the stream. They live from 5 months to 18 months in the wild.

Water voles and their habitat are now fully protected by law.

For more information about water voles, look at these websites:

www.conservancy.co.uk/learn
www.mwhg.org.uk
www.sussexotters.org
www.wwt.org.uk/centre/116/arundel.html
www.wildlifetrusts.org

If you would like to see a water vole in the wild, here is what Harvey the water vole says to you:

- Water voles live in and around water so you need to be careful

- Take an adult with you

- Find out where there is a good place to watch for water voles

- Water voles are quite shy so keep quiet and stand still

- Keep away from the edge of the bank as water voles burrow along the edge of streams and you might squash their burrows

Watching water voles

- Look for signs of water voles such as droppings, cut stems and burrows

- Listen for a 'plop' as they enter the water, a rustling noise like a crisp packet as they run through the vegetation or look for ripples on the water where they are swimming

- Never get into the stream to see them from in the water as this will frighten them too much and could be dangerous for you

- Never try to catch a water vole – it is illegal unless the adult has special permission and a licence

- Always wash your hands before you eat – there may be germs in the habitat that do not harm a water vole but could make you ill

Breed   – to have babies

Burrow   – a tunnel dug into a mud bank
                 where water voles live

Conservation – carefully looking after and
                 protecting an animal, plant or
                 habitat

Drought   – when there has been very little
                 or no rain and the streams dry up

Endangered   – an animal or plant that is in
                 danger of becoming extinct
                 because there are so few left

Flooding   – when there has been a lot of rain
                 and the streams overflow onto
                 the land

Habitat   – a place where an animal chooses
                 to live such as woodland or
                 grassland

Herbivore   – an animal that eats plants

Latrine   – animal toilet

Glossary

Litter	– a number of babies born at the same time
Population	– a group of the same kind of animals that live together
Predator	– an animal that lives by hunting and eating other animals
Prey	– an animal that is hunted and eaten for food by other animals
Scent gland	– special sac of liquid that the animal can use to spread a strong smell on the ground
Territory	– the area belonging to one water vole
Vegetation	– plants
Wetlands	– watery places including marshes, flood meadows, rivers, streams, ditches, ponds, canals, reed beds and saltmarsh

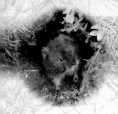

Index